Living LARGE

# A Bear's Life

Sara Antill



PowerKiDS press.
New York

Published in 2012 by The Rosen Publishing Group, Inc.
29 East 21st Street, New York, NY 10010



First Edition

Editor: Jennifer Way
Book Design: Greg Tucker

Photo Credits: Cover, pp. 4, 5, 6, 7, 8, 9 (top), 10, 14 (top, bottom), 15 (top, bottom), 17, 18, 19, 22 Shutterstock.com; p. 11 Darrell Gulin/Getty Images; pp. 12–13 © Wayne Lynch/age fotostock; p. 16 Tom Brakefield/Stockbyte/Thinkstock; p. 20 © Stephen J. Krasemann/age fotostock; p. 21 Daniel Cox/Getty Images.

Library of Congress Cataloging-in-Publication Data

Antill, Sara.
A bear's life / by Sara Antill. — 1st ed.
p. cm. — (Living large)
Includes index.
ISBN 978-1-4488-4977-2 (library binding) — ISBN 978-1-4488-5101-0 (pbk.) —
ISBN 978-1-4488-5102-7 (6-pack)
1. Bears—Life cycles—Juvenile literature. I. Title.
QL737.C27A58 2012
599.78—dc22

2010048487

Manufactured in the United States of America

CPSIA Compliance Information: Batch #WS11PK: For Further Information contact Rosen Publishing, New York, New York at 1-800-237-9932

# Contents

# Meet the Bear

Have you ever seen a bear in the wild? Bears are some of the largest meat-eating animals on Earth! Bears are not born big, though. In fact, when a bear is born, it is about the size of a rat. As it gets older, it becomes bigger and stronger. By the time a bear is about five years old, it is ready to have babies of its own.

The brown bear lives in northern Europe, northern Asia, and in northern North America.

A cub is the earliest stage in the bear's life cycle. This brown bear cub will be fully grown when it is about four to seven years old.

Bears, like all animals, go through different stages of growth. The different stages of an animal's life are called its **life cycle**. Let's find out more about the life of a bear!

# Big and Bigger

Not all bears are the same. There are eight different **species** of bears. The largest of these is the polar bear. Male polar bears can weigh between 660 and 1,760 pounds (299–798 kg). When they stand up, they are almost 10 feet (3 m) tall! The Kodiak bear, a type of brown bear found in Alaska, is almost as big.

Kodiak bears are a subspecies of brown bear that lives in southwestern Alaska. A subspecies is a smaller group within a species.

The sun bear lives in Southeast Asia. Its curled claws help it climb trees.

The smallest bear in the world is the sun bear. These bears stand between 4 and 5 feet (1–1.5 m) tall. They weigh between 60 and 150 pounds (27–68 kg).

# A Perfect Home

Different types of bears live in many parts of the world. Brown bears and American black bears live in Canada and the U.S. states of Alaska, Washington, Wyoming, Montana, and Idaho. Panda bears and sun bears live in Asia.

Different types of bears also live in different **habitats**. Brown bears and

The giant panda lives in mountainous bamboo forests in only a few places in China.

*Right*: Black bears are common in many places in North America.
*Bottom*: This map shows the black bear's range in orange.

American black bears live in mountain forests, meadows, or near rivers. The giant panda lives in forests that are thick with **bamboo**. The polar bear, though, lives in a place with very little plant life. Polar bears spend their lives on large sheets of ice!

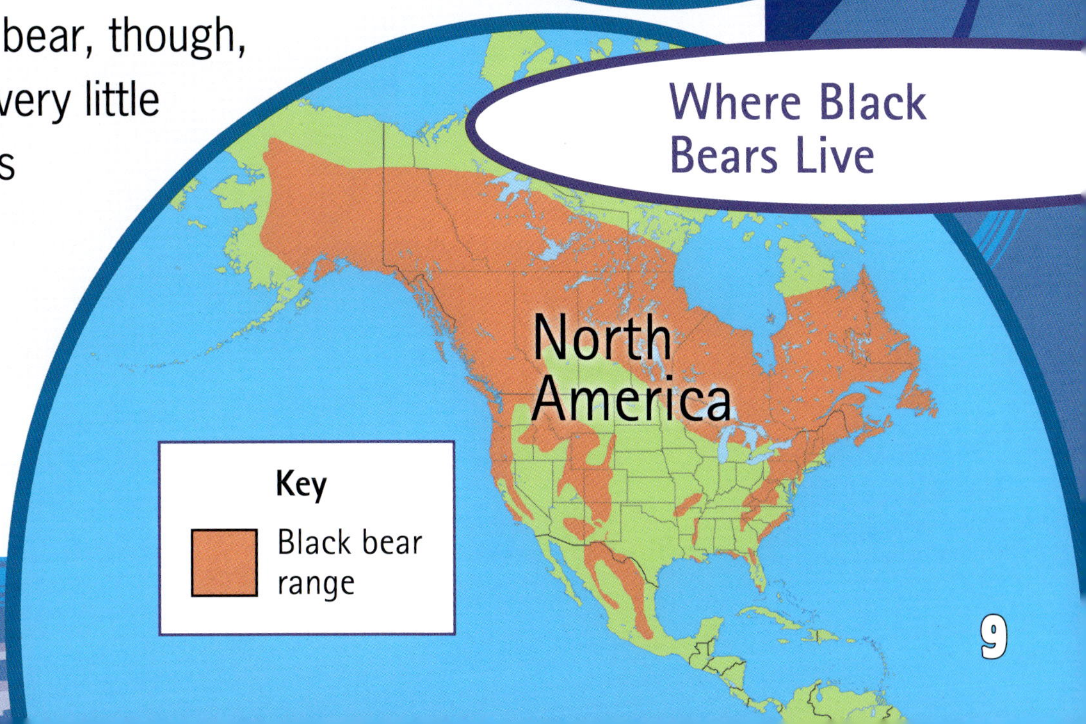

# Food from the Forest

Most bears are **omnivores**. They eat mostly plants, such as leaves, roots, nuts, berries, fruit, and twigs. However, they also eat insects, fish, and other small animals. Sun bears have long tongues that they use to get honey out of beehives.

The grizzly bear is another brown bear subspecies. These bears are omnivores, but they are known for catching fish in rivers.

Polar bears eat mostly seals. Seals have a lot of fat, which the polar bear needs to eat to survive in the icy Arctic.

Unlike other bears, polar bears are **carnivores**. They eat the seals that live in the cold waters around the ice sheets. A polar bear has a very strong sense of smell. It can smell a seal on the ice from 20 miles (32 km) away!

# Time to Sleep

Bears that live in warmer places can stay active all year. However, most bears enter a sleeplike state during the cold winter months. This is called **hibernation**. When a bear is ready to hibernate, it will find a cave or hollow log in which to lie down.

This black bear and her cub are hibernating.

During this time, a bear's heart beats slower to save energy. In the fall, a bear eats extra food to fatten up its body. During its winter hibernation, the bear must live off the fat in its body until it wakes up in the spring.

# Life Cycle of a Bear

1 Baby bears are called cubs. When they are born, they are small, blind, and hairless. Cubs start drinking their mothers' milk as soon as they are born. By the spring, they will weigh 10 to 20 pounds (4.5–9 kg).

4 Bears are ready to **mate** when they are four to five years old. Female bears give birth in the winter, while they are hibernating. When female bears give birth, it is generally to two cubs.

Young cubs leave their dens in spring. Cubs live with their mothers until they are two to three years old. When a mother bear is ready to give birth again, she will chase her older cubs away.

2

An adult bear can eat more than 90 pounds (41 kg) of food a day during the fall! It lives off this extra fat during hibernation.

3

# Cute Cubs

Bears are **mammals**. This means they give birth to live young. Baby bears, called cubs, are born in the winter, while their mother hibernates. In fact, she will not even be awake for their birth! Cubs are very small when they are born. Most weigh between 7 and 20 ounces (198–567 g).

This mother bear is feeding her milk to her cubs.

Mother bears generally give birth to two cubs. However, they sometimes have just one or as many as five cubs!

Cubs drink their mother's milk from the time they are born until they are about six months old. A female bear's milk has a lot of fat in it. This fat helps the young cubs gain lots of weight very quickly.

# Growing and Learning

By their first spring, young cubs weigh between 10 and 20 pounds (4.5–9 kg). When their mother wakes from hibernation, the cubs are ready to leave the den with her. For the next two to three years, a mother bear will teach her cubs how to survive. She will teach them

A mother bear keeps her cubs safe from predators. This brown bear is chasing off a wolf.

This mother bear is teaching her cubs to fish.

how to swim,
climb trees, hunt,
and find food.

A mother bear will also keep her young cubs safe from **predators**. Wolves, mountain lions, and even other adult bears are all a danger to young cubs.

# All Grown Up

When young bears are four to five years old, they are ready to mate. This means that they can have babies of their own. Female bears give birth to cubs every three to four years.

Adult bears will keep growing until they are between 8 and 10 years old. Most bears have **life spans** that are

This is an adult male (right) and female (left) black bear. Except for mothers with cubs, adult bears live alone.

Adult bears come together only to mate. Shown here is an adult grizzly bear.

short compared to the life span of a person. Some species, such as the American black bear, live for only about 10 years in the wild. Others, like the polar bear, live between 15 and 20 years.

# Saving the Bears

Bears like to live away from people. However, there are fewer and fewer places in the world where this is possible. Bears have lost much of their homes to **deforestation**. With less land and food to eat, some bears have started eating from garbage. This can make them very sick. It also brings them closer to where people live, which can be dangerous.

Bears will eat garbage if it is easy for them to get. They can get a taste for people's foods, even when they are not healthy for them.

Many people are trying to help bears, though. Some countries have made laws to stop people from hunting bears and destroying their homes. These laws have kept many bears safe.

# Glossary

**bamboo** (bam-BOO) A thick, woody grass with stems that have a hole in the middle.

**carnivores** (KAHR-neh-vorz) Animals that eat other animals.

**deforestation** (dee-for-uh-STAY-shun) When most of the trees in a forest are cut down.

**habitats** (HA-buh-tats) The surroundings where animals or plants naturally live.

**hibernation** (hy-bur-NAY-shun) Spending the winter in a sleeplike state, with heart rate and breathing rate slowed down.

**life cycle** (LYF SY-kul) The different stages through which a living thing passes from birth to death.

**life spans** (LYF SPANZ) The amount of time that things are alive.

**mammals** (MA-mulz) Warm-blooded animals that have backbones and hair, breathe air, and feed milk to their young.

**mate** (MAYT) To come together to make babies.

**omnivores** (OM-nih-vorz) Animals that eat both plants and animals.

**predators** (PREH-duh-terz) Animals that kill other animals for food.

**species** (SPEE-sheez) One kind of living thing. All people are one species.

# Index



# Web Sites

Due to the changing nature of Internet links, PowerKids Press has developed an online list of Web sites related to the subject of this book. This site is updated regularly. Please use this link to access the list:
www.powerkidslinks.com/livl/bear/